Cally Tales

Cally's Adventures and Those of Her Friends

As told to her Staff,
Sally Humphries

© 2017 Sally Humphries
Printed by CreateSpace, an Amazon.com Company

How It All Began ...

My earliest memory is of bright headlights on a rainy, slick road and a frantic run for cover in grass and weeds. I crashed into a rickety fence and cried my eyes out for my Mama ... but she never came.

The next morning I was coaxed out of the wet weeds by a gentle lady who had seen my frantic run and marked the spot. She brought food, and I was hungry. So I ventured forth and agreed to be rescued. She found me irresistible.

The question, however, was not how irresistible I was, but how adoptable. The gentle lady, who was in the habit of rescuing cats, already had a Maine Coon, and he was not in favor of sharing his space with the likes of me. So she asked a Widow she knew to take me in.

"Don't you think you'd like a kitten to keep you company?" was the way she phrased it.

But the Widow really didn't think so. She thought she would be busy visiting grandchildren. Nevertheless, she said she would pray about it.

"Would you hurry?" the Cat Rescuer quickly replied. "My husband is just around the corner from your house and he is bringing the Calico kitten to show you."

The Widow was too polite to hang up ... fortunately. She said instead: "Well, I suppose ... maybe ... It won't hurt to take a look."

When I arrived and was handed off to her, I snuggled up and licked her arm. In short, I was absolutely irresistible. And that's how I went from the wet weeds to a comfortable house and regular meals in the short space of 48 hours.

How I Got My Name and How I Earn My Keep

Since I am a Calico, Cally was a logical name. In case you can't tell, my fur is a beautiful blend of bronze and white and honey colors. I have four white paws, which I meticulously wash daily, a white bib which makes me look like a maitre d', and a freckle on my nose. I like my name and I generally approve of the whole deal. However, being a charming, cuddly, playful kitten only gets you so far. Eventually I had to buckle down and earn my keep.

My home was on a wooded lot and had a basement and garage, so mice flocked to the site in military formations. (Or so it seemed.) Instinctively I knew this was a problem, and I was the one who must solve it.

No one trained me in "mousing;" they didn't have to. The first time I saw a mouse, I knew what to do. Stalk, capture, and dispose of. In no time, I made a dent in the mouse population, and the Widow was pleased.

She knew when I disappeared in the basement for an extended period and only came upstairs at mealtime, I was attending to business. Then when I reappeared for lap sits and bedtime cuddles, she came to the basement to get the body count and see where I had put the deceased.

Sometimes I laid them out Hollywood-style between the oil tank and the furnace. Sometimes there was no trace, not even a whisker ... and I gave no hints. My motto was, and still is, "Keep 'em guessing." I learned this from my cousin, Precious, who lives in Indiana.

Meet Cousin Precious

Precious is a tuxedo cat, which means she always seems to be formally dressed, either for dinner at a fancy fish restaurant or an evening at the opera. Since she lives with a musical human, I assume the opera. Precious said "keep 'em guessing" was the secret to a long life. I wrote it on the wall next to my litter box and studied on it.

Hence the other night the Widow passed the laundry basin in the basement and saw a strange looking string in the drain. She pulled it, then screeched like a teenager. The "string", of course, was the tail of a mouse. A dead mouse, but nevertheless a mouse who was head down in the open drain. How could that happen? She was in a state of shock and wonder. She wanted details. My official response was, "No comment." Like Precious says, "It's best to keep 'em guessing."

The Hair Ball Thing

Precious also gave me good advice on the hair ball thing. Hair balls, of course, are ho-hums to cats but stomach turners to humans.

But I decided cleanliness was a virtue, and if licking myself clean from ear to paw produced hair balls, so be it. If the Widow chose to gag over hair balls, that was her problem. I stated my case. Then she stated hers... which was no hair balls, no matter what.

A mutual friend suggested a compromise might be the FURminator, which is a fancy stainless steel comb that gets rid of shedding hair. Probably designed by a hair-ball-gagging human, I thought, but at least not bitter-tasting medicine. Nevertheless, Rule 42 in the Cat Manual says, "Never try a new thing ... without an okay from some feline older and wiser."

So I emailed Precious. Behold. She not only knew about the FURminator, but had eons of experience and thought it was better than a fancy massage at a pricey cat salon. Since Precious is not only my cousin, but also the Senior Cat Advisor to The World At Large, I decided to try this new thing.

I love it! I even roll from side to side to get a full treatment.

Precious in a Huff

While we are on the subject of Precious, I must mention that wise as she is, she also has a temper. Only last week she was in a huff because her Mama human would not let her romp on the keyboard of the computer. With ears laid back in attack mode, Precious jumped to the nearby copy machine. Copies came flying out, gears rumbled, lights flashed.

She planned to paper the floor, walls, and ceiling with copies, then march out the door with a triumphant, "So there!" Her Mama, however, pushed the "off" button and ended the drama. Privately Precious told me she dreams of having a banner over her litter box that says simply, "Don't mess with Precious, the Copy Cat."

I Was Inspired to Try Leaping

Hearing of Precious's adventures with the copy machine inspired me to try leaping. What caught my eye was a magnificent ceramic eagle on a shelf about ten feet up. Birds, of course, are part of my DNA, and this one was a whopper. I yearned for a closer look. I climbed onto the wing chair under the shelf, studying my prey from every angle. Finally I launched from the top edge of the chair.

It was a magnificent leap worthy of Olympic gold for style and speed, but alas, the shelf gave way and crashed my prey into a hundred pieces. I got a bong on the head, but I was far from discouraged. In fact, I was invigorated! I had my first real taste of leaping, and I liked it!

Soon I was on the hunt for bigger leaps from higher and more daring launch pads. Eureka! I discover the loft on the second floor above the living room. Probably 18 feet up. I walked the ledge of the loft every day for a week or so, deciding how and what and where.

What caught my eye this time was a porthole window about four feet away. Why? Simple. Because I could see tree tops and birds in motion. Why go DOWN when I could go OVER and have a spectacular view? So I launched. Needless to say it was a daredevil leap of incredible skill and timing. The Widow nearly had a heart attack when she spied me 18 feet up on a 5-inch sill.

"Okay, Whisker Face," she said dramatically, "how do you propose to get back?" After a meaningful pause, I looked down as if to say, "Who says I'm going back?"

Quick as a hare, she ran downstairs and rearranged the furniture … presumably to provide me with a soft landing. Or perhaps to avoid an ugly stain on the carpet.

I was, of course, stringing her along. I knew what I intended to do, and I knew she had no idea. In fact, she was so rattled, she emptied a large basket and leaned over the loft ledge, suggesting I jump in it. I gave her the "You Must Be Out of Your Mind" look. Time passed. Finally, I heard her mutter in frustration, "There's always another cat to adopt."

BAM. In the blink of an eye, I was back on the loft ledge, purring sweetly, "Let's not talk replacement. Let's talk dinner. I'm famished with all this leaping about."

I decided to end my leaping career on that high note. Don't mess with success. Rule #43 in the Cat Manual.

Being an Inside Cat...

It was decided that I would be an "inside cat." I had no vote in the matter.

The Widow had heard the scary cry of the fisher cat on her walk around the block. She had seen a young bear amble across our street in daytime and heard the night-time cry of the coyote. She knew firsthand that a neighbor, three houses down on the next street, lost her "indoor-outdoor cat" and had spent days wandering our streets calling, "Kitty, Kitty, Kitty," with absolutely no reply. Case closed.

Outdoor life was too risky, she said. I was lucky to be rescued from the wet weeds beside that busy road where I was dumped as a mere babe. Why push my luck? Okay, Okay, I said to myself.

HOWEVER, winter came, and we had an awesome snowstorm. I was captivated by the thought of exploring this white stuff. When the Widow opened the door to measure the snow, I impulsively leaped into the drift and hopped about like a kangaroo. She ran for her boots, thinking she would have to chase me around the deck.

I was looking forward to a merry chase, but my tummy began to freeze up. So I reversed course and headed back to the warm house... about the time she reappeared with boots in hand. We haven't spoken of this incident since.

Being an "inside cat" isn't really so bad, I said to myself. I can stick with my email friends, and perhaps venture onto Facebook.

My Friend Boo

I met Boo on Facebook and soon discovered we had some things in common; namely, we both began our kittenhood as orphans.

While my story began on a busy road in wet weeds, Boo remembers tall grass and noisy streets. She was a hungry and frightened orphan. Then she wandered into a back yard and heard an interesting conversation coming from an open window. It was an older cat voice and a human one ... talking to each other. The more she listened, the more she liked what she heard.

With a soft and pathetic meow, she presented her case for adoption... and dinner. The Mama human looked her over and voted "maybe." The problem was housing. There was yet another cat in the house and the Mama human had no idea how the newbie would be accepted. Would it be "love and kisses" or "scratch her eyes out?" There would be temporary housing in the office and a wait-and-see period.

As for what to name the newcomer, the Daddy human, whose office it was, liked Yogi Bear cartoons and kept asking, "Hey, Boo Boo, you want to steal a picinick basket?" She had no idea how to answer that. But since her situation was way better than the tall grass and noisy streets, she decided to hunker down, wait things out, and answer to Boo.

Boo was finally accepted and today her family calls her The Treat-monger because nothing distracts her when she is after her evening treat. She does lap leaps, neck wraps, as well as TV screen blocks and computer keyboard walks. It's heavy duty "in your face" behavior until she has her way.

And when she gets what she wants, she does a role reversal, sits on her haunches like a squirrel, and daintily nibbles her handful of treats, as if she were the Queen.

Speaking of the Queen

I hear that Precious lives like a queen. That is, she has her own place mat, her own dish, and her own high chair at the dinner table. And when she asks for Brie, she gets it.

However, if the truth be known, Precious mainly lives on baby food meat. The kitchen staff calls it "senior food," but only in hushed tones, because Precious is very word sensitive. She likes to think she is still a high school pompom girl.

As for me, I eat whatever I can smooze from my Widow. When I first saw yogurt in her dish, I wanted some in mine. It was the same with her bran muffin. Her turkey. Her salmon. Her cheese, her eggs. Just not her kale. Yuk. Personally, I think kale should be fed only to chipmunks, who don't seem to care what they eat.

How I Became a Fat Cat

I admit to becoming a fat cat. And I did it in the usual way ... eating too much and too often. Early on, I encouraged my human to believe she couldn't overfeed me. After all, I was not a dog. I was a cat and would only eat when I was hungry. Snicker. Snicker.

It wasn't long, however, before there was a hammock of fat swinging between my four legs. I was off to the vet for a weigh in and a special diet food.

Three months later, the hammock was still swinging, and my diet was changed to something with "fat cat" in the title. I was mortified to have my problem "out there" in plain view on a cat food bag.

Mortified or not, nothing changed. Then Boo's humans came to my rescue and suggested a new brand of cat food that was mostly protein. They called it "Mouse In A Can." I liked the sound of that. And sure enough, my pudge began to fade away. I breathed a sigh of relief.

Boo and her sisters, Bones and Deena, were also eating "Mouse In A Can." It is so reassuring to have a support group. We all are dreaming of becoming slim and trim, like the glamour girls on the cat food cans.

The Back Story on Bones

Time out to explain more about Bones. She was brought into the family before Boo, and in much the same way. She heard Deena and her Mama human conversing at the open window, and it drew her like a magnet. Bones was desperate for a home and food. She was, in fact, a walking skeleton that might have blown away in a strong wind if she hadn't been weighed down by a belly full of kittens near term. What human could refuse such a spunky little mother?

She was immediately adopted and given all she could eat. When the birthing finally began, five little gray balls of fur arrived, wiggling and hungry for their mama's milk, but there wasn't nearly enough.

Bones admits to getting teary-eyed thinking about the two that didn't make it, even though she and her humans gave it their all.

Time passed and then came the day when her three wiggly mischief makers were strong enough to be on their own. What to do in an overcrowded household? Fortunately, there were many potential owners, so Bones went into street-smart mode to make the best selections. Does she miss her babies? Of course she does. But life goes on.

The good news is she is no longer a walking skeleton, but a ravishing beauty of gray and white and black. Although she is still fondly called Bones, and she answers the call, it's probably because she is too shy to speak up and risk offending her food suppliers.

Update on Boo and Deena

Today Boo still has an adorable little baby face. But it's attached to the body of a Maine Coon. Even her vet, who surely has seen most everything, was caught off guard. "There's a lot of cat in there," he finally managed to say, looking into her carrier.

Meanwhile, Deena, the one responsible for attracting Boo and Bones at the open window in Alabama, is still "talking" a blue streak. But no longer at an open window. The family moved north and rented a condo to be near grandchildren. So everything is high up and different. Deena, for one, is lobbying for another move back to the ground floor. It might happen.

Not All My Friends Are Hardship Cases...
Some Came from Orphanages

There's Gracie, a sassy Indiana kitten, who probably never knew hunger. Gracie was raised in an Orphanage (Animal Shelter) where food was always available. How much she got of what, however, was a matter of skill. Since Gracie was full of sass and hiss, she held her own.

The end game at the Orphanage, however, was to get "adopted." This required some salesmanship. So between meals the Orphanage residents practiced their adoption roles. Some cast themselves as cute and cuddly, adorable and charming. Others went for sad and pitiful. The goal was to close the sale.

On Mondays, Tuesdays, and Wednesdays, Gracie put her sass and hiss aside and practiced being "adorable and charming." On Thursdays, Fridays, and Saturdays, she played the role of "pitiful and sad". Great performances, but no cigar. Then one Saturday she overheard a potential owner say the cat who let you hold it in your arms like a baby would make the best pet. So she immediately became an expert at flopping on her back, begging to be held like a baby, while softly purring and making eye contact.

Within days, she was adopted and taken to her first home. Once there, she made it her immediate goal to rule the roost. She never doubted that the sun rose and set when she told it to. And she meant to convince her humans of this fundamental truth.

She was a black and white, and that's the way she viewed her world. All black, or all white. No middle ground. Imagine her surprise when her humans went back to the Orphanage and brought home another black and white to be her playmate. Humans call that being blindsided.

Another Black and White

The playmate was named Jakey and he was adopted via the same technique as Gracie. He allowed himself to be held like a baby so Gracie's humans would consider him an ideal choice. For his part, his new home was everything he dreamed of … peaceful and quiet with a large front window for watching dogs and cars and bicycles go by.

Gracie sometimes joined him at the window. At first, he thought she shared his love for peace and quiet. But it soon became clear that she was only sizing him up for projects she had on her "to do" list. When she got around to describing her first project, his response was a disinterested yawn. Her response to his response was a wild dance of swats and hisses.

Mercy, he reasoned, she has had too much catnip, but discovering none in the house, he ambled off to his secret hiding place for a snooze. And so it was with Jakey and Gracie until the time Baby Zeke was born.

Enter Baby Zeke

When Baby Zeke came home from the hospital, things changed. Gracie and Jakey put their differences aside to present a united front against the intruder. They couldn't decide what was most irritating. Was it having their sleep disturbed in the wee hours of the morning? Was it having their meals delayed for hours? Or was it having to step carefully and slowly into a loaded litter box that wasn't scooped as often as it used to be?

The humans said, "Sorry," and looked "Sorry," and sounded "Sorry", but at the end of the day, Gracie and Jakey felt unloved and under-appreciated. By unanimous vote, they wanted the newcomer sent packing. They assumed he came from the Orphanage where they came from and was returnable.

Precious Gives Wise Counsel

Precious, Senior Cat Advisor to The World At Large, weighed in at this point. She lived across the street and knew all about Baby Zeke. She also knew the pecking order in households.

She summoned the miffed kittens and laid down the law. "Listen up," she commanded. "You need to get over it, and you need to get on with it. Life is short." Lowering her voice, she concluded sternly, "And don't lay a paw on him, or your life will be shorter." Precious was never one to mince words.

Learning To Live With It

So Jakey and Gracie keep trying to "get over it" and to "get on with it." This is particularly hard for Gracie because Lap Time with the Mama human used to be hers exclusively, but now Baby Zeke is there. It feels like time share. Very unsettling.

And Jakey? Well, now that Baby Zeke has learned to walk and is picking up speed every day, Jakey needs to watch where he steps to avoid collisions. Gone are the days of his not-a-care-in-the-world household strolls. Very unsettling.

Precious Reminds Me of Max

Now that I think of it, Precious reminds me of Max, my neighborhood hero and guidance counselor. Not long after I settled in with the Widow, Max came by to get acquainted. He had heard that I was being groomed as an "inside cat" and wanted to offer his sympathy.

He knew the chipmunks would torment me. They would parade back and forth on my front step, close by my screen door, to taunt me with the chipmunk song, "Nah-nah-nah, can't catch me. I'm a chipmunk and I am free."

Sure enough. They did what he said. I was soon totally frustrated. Max advised me to keep my cool. Life was short, and chipmunks were a dime a dozen.

And to help me adjust to my "inside" life, Max entertained me with stories. He told me about Oliver, the high-tech cat who lived two doors down.

He told me about the wild turkeys that flew in and out of yards as if they personally owned them. And the woodchucks who ate most everything in sight. And the skunks. He knew some of them by name.

But his most hair-raising story was about a mountain lion seen walking our street in the moonlight. A retired police officer, four doors down, reported the sighting and who could doubt the word of an officer of the law trained in accurate reporting? Maybe Max was pulling my tail on the mountain lion. I can't be sure. I can only say his stories slowly made me more content being an "inside cat."

Mixed in with Max's stories were his flirtatious remarks. He said things that made me blush. But he also became a trusted friend. He listened to my rants about the uppity chipmunks.
There was one in particular, Mr. Chips, who really needled me. In

fact, he made me so mad I nearly split a whisker. Then one morning I went to my door and, behold, at the foot of the steps was Uppity Mr. Chips, dead as a doornail, stiff as a starched shirt, a perfectly laid out corpse. I knew who had "done him in" and I was ready to follow Max to the moon.

But We Lost Max

It happened so suddenly. One day he was here; the next, he was gone. Well, not in the forever sense. Just in the neighborhood. Oliver, the cat who lives two doors down, texted me that Max's humans sold their house and moved out.

He said there were claw marks in the driveway about the size of Max's. Oliver thinks he was taken by force. But who knows … he might have been bribed. He didn't like to miss a meal. I guess we'll never know unless we get a text.

On the other hand, knowing Max, he is more likely to communicate by jungle drum. Or maybe he will reappear and give us the full story. I miss Max.

Oliver Misses Max Too

I think Oliver misses Max almost as much as I do. They were buddies. And I hear that because of Max's disappearance, Oliver made a career change from "mouse patrols" to watching TV shows and studying computer screens for hours. Then one day he decided to become an expert in the anatomy of ears. Cat ears, that is. Why would he be interested in any other kind?

In a recent conversation, he informed me that I have 32 muscles for each of my ears. Imagine that! And I can move each ear independently of the other. In fact, I can point my ears in one direction and my body in another. I might have picked up on that if I had stood in front of the mirror and studied it. Nevertheless, it's nice of Oliver to let me know.

Of course, I knew about laid back ears. They are cat language for being miffed. When I lay back my ears, it's just before I sunk my teeth into a human's arm.

But it was those little pockets at the bottom of cat ears that I always wondered about. When I asked Max about his, he told me they were "glove compartments" where he kept valuables. Since he said this with a straight face, I believed him. But now I'm not so sure. Oliver says they have a special name, but no one knows what they are for.

To Pass the Time Without Max

To pass the time without Max's visits, I resorted to the old-fashioned Tail Chase. I do my best version in the doorway to the bathroom. Just a personal preference. It's not in the Rule Book.

Tail Chase a lá Cally is to pretend not to look at my tail, while looking at it over my shoulder. When the time seems right, I pounce on it and seem to mean business. Sometimes I give it a bit of a nip, as though it belonged to someone else. Other times I throw in a dramatic hiss to jazz up the moment before the pounce. Always I end up letting the poor thing loose. Otherwise there wouldn't be anything to chase.

My Widow gets excited about Tail Chase a lá Cally even though she doesn't understand why I do it. What she likes is that I'm getting some EXERCISE … and not sleeping my life away. To encourage me in the EXERCISE department, she once tried the laser pen light. Dreadful.

The Folly of the Laser Pen

Oliver says most cat families buy a laser pen light, thinking to play high tech tricks on the gullible among us. I think this is both true and shameful. Oliver agrees.

Both of us suspect the laser pen industry was sinking fast when some advertising wizard decided to pitch it to cat owners to make their pets look foolish.

I admit to being victimized by the laser pen light. In fact, I was on the verge of going batty chasing that red point of light up and down the wall, back and forth across the floor. Then I had an "aha" moment.

Why should I chase a light, I said to myself, that I can't put a paw on? When I expend energy chasing something, I want to be able to catch it. Put a paw on it. Hold it down. Conquer it.

Call me an old fogy, but I would much rather chase a humble twist tie from a bag of muffins.

Boo Rolls Vitamins

Boo feels the same way. Why chase a light when there are all kinds of interesting things to chase on the kitchen counter top? Like vitamins, which are off limits, but irresistible. They roll so nicely and they drop off the edge almost silently.

These are vitamins that are "out of their bottles" and ready for consumption. So it's a short game that usually ends with a glare of disapproval from her Mama.

Boo has already been subjected to more than one lecture about "the cost of vitamins." Since she doesn't know the cost of anything, and certainly not vitamins, the lecture is meaningless.

She is always looking for a new small thing that will roll nicely and drop to the floor silently. It could be a ballpoint pen or a bottle cap or a cough drop. Boo thinks each of these objects is designed particularly for her enjoyment. She is completely oblivious to remarks like,

"Where did that pen go? It was just here."

Why, she wonders, do her housemates give her toys with whistles and bells and feathers, when a simple bottle cap would keep her happy for hours?

Walking the Kitchen Counter

Walking the kitchen counter is something we all do for entertainment. And it drives our housemates crazy. At parties, they spend eons of time asking each other how to get us to stop. All I can say is that some of my best friends are counter walkers ... and they resist all efforts to kick the habit.

Personally, I am an intermittent counter walker. At times I take to the kitchen counter when the Widow is bedding down for the night and not paying attention. Sometimes I get caught in the act and have to quickly jump down, giving the classic cat excuse that I didn't know I was up there.

I have also been known to do a counter walk when the Widow has dinner guests, just to be a brat. I know there is nothing she can say to convince her guests my presence on her kitchen counter is unusual. They think it is my everyday behavior and they are horrified. I think it's poetic justice for not being allowed to eat what they eat.

Boo, however, has never been selective about her counter walks. She hangs out on the counter most all the time and doesn't bother with excuses. As the youngest in her family, she claims it's a privilege of her youth.

Her older sisters, Deena and Bones, have been known to suck breath in disbelief that Boo gets away with such outrageous acts.

Gracie Has a Unique Counter Walk Twist

Precious recently emailed me that Gracie, who lives close to her, has added a new twist to counter walking that is truly ingenious. She waits until her Mama human is busy with the dishes, then she does a quiet counter sneak followed by a swift leap to the top of the fridge. The only word that comes close to describing Gracie's feeling of accomplishment is … SMUG. After all, she towers over everyone in the room. She is out of reach. And she can choose to catch a nap or spend the time thinking things through.

Warm Places

The top of the fridge is also a warm place, and we all like warm places. I know if I find a patch of sunshine anywhere in the house, I'm on it in the blink of an eye. On gloomy, cold days I wiggle under the bed covers for naps. Breathing never seems as important as warmth ... in the short term.

On frigid nights I snuggle with the Widow. It's especially wonderful because she puts a warm rice bag under the covers. I heard of a young cat who was housed on a screened-in porch ... outside, mind you ... but given an electric heating pad to bed down with. She was said to be happy.

Boo brags that she has found the absolute best of warm places. It's in the clothes dryer on top of warm towels. She gives it a five star rating, even though there are risks involved. She says she learned about the risks from another cat who fell asleep on warm towels, and then was spun around on the dry cycle.

Herbie in the Dryer

I bet that was Herbie because I remember hearing the story of his "day after." It is said he looked disheveled, and his eyes were not entirely focused. His first-person account is that the incident happened late at night when he thought the household was asleep. Most were. But not all. The Mama human had come home late and found a note asking her to finish drying the clothes. So she closed the dryer door and pushed the "ON" button. Hearing the Boom, Thud, Thud, she is reported to have muttered, "Oh rats! I told those kids not to put their tennis shoes in the dryer."

When she opened the door to remove the shoes, she was astonished to find a shell-shocked Herbie. His fur was badly rumpled, his whiskers wilted, and his eyes rolling.

She hugged him, kissed him, and told him how sorry she was. He seemed to accept her apologies, although he was never quite as cordial.

Actually, this was not the first misfortune for Herbie. I have it on good authority that as a kitten, he lived in an apartment with a zany couple who kept him stuffed in a cupboard most of the time. This affected his emotional life and made him very moody.

Strangers in the House

There's a whole section in the Cat Manual titled "Strangers in the House." It taught me to be sensitive to non-family members who come thru the door. Some are invited, of course, but others are repairmen or somebody selling something.

Oh, the smells these Strangers bring! You wonder why I head straight for their shoes and sniff like a hound? Well, practically speaking, their shoes are close to my nose. That's one thing. The other is, shoes are very "down to earth," so to speak. Shoes bring in grass smells and dirt smells, and sometimes squashed ant, grasshopper, beetle and dog smells. Shoe smells give "inside cats" like me, a world of information about life on the other side of my door.

I digress. The real question is: How long will the Strangers stay? And then, how inconvenienced will I be by the visit?

My favorite Stranger is the "in and out" one. The shorter the visit the less likely I am to be denied my favorite spot on the sofa, or on the bed, or freedom to walk the counter.

If the visitors bring luggage, I know I'm in for curtailments. If they bring luggage and children, heaven help me. Tail grabs, for sure.

Even worse is the Stranger who claims an allergy to cats. This means exile in the basement or bathroom for the duration of the visit.

But the very worst of the worst is the Stranger who arrives with or without luggage and children, but with a DOG. This means "war games" and there's no help for it.

Empty House Time

Most of us delight in having the house to ourselves. When I hear the Widow close the door and start her car, I head for the front window to make sure she is really leaving. When she sees me at the window, she thinks I'm depressed about being left behind. Nothing could be further from the truth. I tremble with excitement. I have the house to myself.

My first move is to pick up my stuffed frog by the scruff of his neck and take him to the kitchen and then to the living room fireplace. He seems to delight in viewing the oven and the fireplace tongs. I have no idea why.

Sometimes I take my stuffed bear on the tour of the basement. He is fascinated with the dryer and the furnace. After all this hauling up and down the stairs, I'm ready for some fun time with my ball of red yarn.

Yarn winds nicely in and out of table and chair legs. The problem is winding it up again before the Widow comes back. Usually I can't and I get a heavy sigh of disapproval. Still, there's nothing like the freedom of Empty House Time.

Boo and Her Sisters Have a Different Take

Boo and her sisters at the Condo have a different take on Empty House Time. As soon as they are sure they are alone, it's on your mark, get set, GO to a place that's off limits normally. Not for mischief, but for a nap. One takes the Mama human's favorite spot on the couch. Another goes for the comfy recliner normally claimed by the Daddy human. Even the shy Bones, who loves hiding places in general, roams about and chooses a napping spot that is unique to the Empty House situation.

Empty House Time, according to Boo, is also good for pouncing on desk chairs that spin around. The trick to a long ride is to get a little speed going before the pounce. Trust Boo to think of that.

She also likes to burrow under those funny little throw rugs that seem to have no purpose and to balance them on her head to do a "walk about" ... as if she were Australian. (I do that too.)

The sound of the door opening means it's time to vacate the forbidden spots and stop all unauthorized activities. The race is on to appear normal.

Play Time is Different

Play time is different than unauthorized activities in Empty House Time. Play time is what we do when our human family is watching. Or could be watching.

Most of us pretend we are race cars at the Indy 500... which means without warning, we go from zero to 200 (or more) in and out of rooms, up and over things. We don't need to hear, "Gentlemen, start your engines." We just GO ... GO ... GO, as if our tails were on fire. Anything or anyone who gets in the way is likely to be toppled, including children and the elderly. No discrimination.

Boo tells me that being high speed race cars is thrilling at her house because of Deena and Bones. Each goes at full speed in a different direction. To keep from crashing into each other, they dart up and over obstacles and send books and footstools and even scratching towers flying. Whoopee!

Play Time with a Mouse

Much as I like galloping thru the house like a high speed race car, I also like "mouse drops." In this play time maneuver, I appear upstairs, carrying a mouse in my mouth and looking like a victorious hunter. The Widow is horrified and wonders why I am bringing a dead mouse upstairs instead of leaving it in the basement between the furnace and the oil tank. "Cally Humphries," she says in icy tones, "take that mouse downstairs! This instant! March!"

That's when I drop the very much alive mouse and let it scamper away. Now we have shrieks, threats, and glaring looks. All to no avail. The mouse is behind the bookcase and out of reach. If he makes a move, however, I'm on him. The Widow has no worries, but that doesn't keep her from worrying. I'm in complete control, and I love it!

Sometimes the Widow Wins One

I'm remembering the time I looked up from my nap to see a full-sized lion walking thru the dining room. I froze in place and thought the end was near. Here was the King of Beasts right in my own house. Probably looking for me. I considered all my options, then I sunk into the carpet and snaked my way, inch by inch, to my hiding spot under the sofa. Surely this was one place a full-sized lion could not go.

Alas! I heard the Widow talking on her cell. "It fits just fine," she

said, "and if I wear my brown slippers, I think that will solve the paw problem."

You guessed it. The Widow had consented to wear a Lion's costume at the autumn festival to help draw customers to the Lion's Club BBQ. Chalk one up for the Widow.

Going to the Vet

The first time I made the trip to the vet, I was an innocent and trusting kitten. I rode in a picnic basket and enjoyed the ride. By the time we made the second trip, the Widow had invested in a medium-size carrier with mesh windows so I could see out, although there was nothing to see but the dashboard and door handles. I handled it all so well that she had visions of the two of us taking cross-country trips. She would drive, and I would ride shotgun.

In fact, we took several practice spins around town. Then my native instincts kicked in. Wait a minute, I said to myself, I am a cat and cats are bound by the rules of the Cat Manual to vigorously protest being put into a Cat Carrier. It's what we do. Hence, the battle of the Cat Carrier began.

Cat Carrier Warfare

Whenever the Cat Carrier is sighted, I begin mapping my strategy. There are three beds to hide under, a sofa, chairs with skirts, and closets. I have a route in mind and when the Widow approaches, I go from one to another as quick as a hare. Several times she canceled the appointment because I wore her out. The last time, however, was different.

After the initial chase under beds, sofa, and chairs, the Widow pretended to give up and take a nap. I pumped my paw in the air. Another victory. But, no sooner had I closed my eyes to nap then she ambled from room to room quietly closing the doors. Next she offered me my favorite treat. I thought I had won. When she picked me up, I wiggled free. But with all those closed doors, I had nowhere to go.

She soon had me in the "stuffing in" position. However, the carrier's wire door came to my rescue and gave her a gouge on the forearm. Blood gushed. She had to tend to her wound, and I was on the loose again. I think she called the vet and cut a deal to forget the appointment time and just show up as circumstances permitted. I didn't hear the full conversation.

Truly I was concerned for the Widow's blood loss. Would she still be able to tend to my needs? I was in the mood to lick her wound and show compassion. We met on the stairs, and I surrendered. Into the cat carrier I went. She is now MY Widow.

Reconsidering My Cat Carrier Stance

My negative ancestral instincts about cat carriers may have to be reconsidered. Recently I heard of cousins and nieces and nephews who ride to the vet snuggled in one human's lap while the other drives. An idea worth considering since laps are generally warmer than the floors of cat carriers. And who doesn't love a warm place?

The only problem with lap rides is that there is too much to see. Trees, big scary trucks, and telephone poles whiz by at incredible speeds, causing most of us to toss our cookies. The wise thing to do is to close the eyes and pretend to nap.

Hats Off to Sebastian

I did hear about a very intelligent tabby named Sebastian who rode to his vet's in the passenger seat (with no seat belt) and no warm lap for comfort. Just straight on, so to speak. Sebastian was diabetic, and he had no choice about making the trip often. So he did it with style. In fact, when his housemate opened the car door, he walked straight to the vet's door with a manly stride and never once bolted. He knew what he had to do, and he faced it like a man.

Further, he was no coward when it came to his insulin shots. I might have made my Widow chase me down every 12 hours, or I might have faked seizures. But not Sebastian. He "manned up" to it. It's possible he is the one who originated the saying, "It is what it is."

Boo, Bones, and Deena Take Car Travel in Stride

Boo, Bones, and Deena think nothing of car travel to the vet ... or anywhere else. They have spent nights in motels and days in cars. Each has her own carrier and each her own travel style. Mostly it's sleep, yawn, and stretch on the road, but once they hit the motel room and the carrier doors open, SHAZAM! Boo explores her new surroundings and romps. Bones finds a dark and secret place to hide. Deena arches her back, scratches her ears, and takes a leisurely bath. All eat a bit and take a turn at the litter box.

Bedding down for the night is no problem. Any warm, soft spot not directly under the blast of the air conditioner is acceptable. The Front Desk thinks their feline guests spend the night in their carriers,

but that is delusional. The room door is plastered with Do Not Disturb signs and locked up tight at an early hour for good reason.

In the morning, the cat carriers are lined up in the bathtub with the door ends up. On the count of three, one human grabs the closest cat, while the other pops open the door and assists with the stuffing in process. Then, on to number two. The very shy Bones is always last because she has to be pried out of some secret place.

Then it's another day on the road and another night at a motel. Speaking for the traveling trio, Deena wants the world to know that traveling with cats is a breeze compared to traveling with children. The three main advantages she mentions are no potty stops, no fussing for an ice cream, and no whining about "How much longer?"

Cat Talk

Deena is the most vocal of my friends. She can carry on a decent conversation with her Mama human which both seem to understand. That's how she "marketed" herself at the Orphanage (Animal Shelter). "Talking" brought attention and earned her a comfortable home.

And that's how Boo and Bones found their way into the family. It was Deena's conversation at the open window in Alabama. She doesn't do "words" exactly, but she uses her voice in a sliding scale of sounds which answer her Mama human's questions in some mysterious way.

I consider myself semi-vocal. I have no problem letting my Widow know I am hungry or that I want to go to the garage for a mouse patrol. I'm heavy into meowing and light on purring. My favorite word is "hmph" which either means "I agree" or "Just do it."

I am also known for my "sighs." I have no idea where I learned them or exactly what they mean. According to my Widow, they slip out, mostly when I'm napping, and I don't even know it. Maybe Oliver can do a study on "sighs" after he finishes with "ears," but in the meantime, I'll just let them come and go as they please.

I hear Gracie does "chirps." Whatever those are. And Precious has a Meow language that is unique. She does short meows, long meows, and nondescript meows that are like "hmmmms." She also growls when she is out of sorts.

Behold! My Widow and I Are Making a Move

It's true. Both my Widow and I have been working ourselves to exhaustion these past few years. Me with the perpetual mouse invasion from the woods nearby and she with the upkeep of the lawn, the flower gardens, and the house maintenance in general. Like Precious advised the Indiana kittens, Life is short. Why waste it on big houses and witless mice?

So she selling our big house and building a small place in VA, attached to her daughter's BIG house. No basement, no mice. I like that. I've had my fill of mice. I need a break.

I just broke the "we're moving" news to Oliver, and he seems to be taking it in stride. He says we can email and text, and it will probably make our relationship even more "fulfilling." I'm not sure what Oliver means by "fulfilling."

Bones and Deena only rolled their eyes. They have been through many moves and prefer to remain silent and let me find out about moving on my own. I hardly know what to make of that.

Chaos Is What Moving Means

Now I know.

Moving is CHAOS.

Nothing is where it was.

Boxes are everywhere.

Paper is rattling. I can't find a decent place to take a nap. I am constantly being coaxed into "exile" in the basement. There is the unfamiliar sound of feet overhead, coming and going. Strange voices. Weird noises.

And what in the basement is of interest to me? All that remains is the furnace, the oil tank, the washer and dryer, and my litter box. But I am resourceful.

With fresh morning litter, I can create sand dune sculptures. Sometimes after a hardy breakfast or lunch, I can do a mountain peak or two. It all depends on the material at hand.

My Longest Exile

The Yard Sale was my longest time in exile. Oliver, my friend two doors down, advised me to "take heart." Yard Sale Exile, he said, was for my own protection. My Widow was only concerned for my safety. All kinds of people come to Yard Sales. Even catnappers. I don't know where Oliver gets his information, but he seems to know things.

My second longest exile was the day the packers came to load up the U-Haul. Thump. Thud. Thud. But no big crashes that I could detect. The next morning I was lowered into my Cat Carrier, and we departed the neighborhood with flags flying. I think I saw Oliver watching from his front window, perhaps with a tear in his eye. I must admit I will miss him … somewhat.

On the Road

Deena advised that the best way to travel is to "zone out." So I curled up like a wooly worm and zoned. When we made our first stop for food and "necessities," I pretended to be asleep. Then the thought came to me, What if I could do this entire 620 miles, two-day trip, in the car with no food, no water, and no litter box breaks? Surely that would give me a reputation for incredible Determination and Momentous Self-Discipline. I imagined I would be the talk of the Cat World for years to come. Oliver would hear of my amazing feat on his favorite TV show and text me of his undying adoration.

That night in the motel room, my growling stomach almost changed my mind. In fact, I took a sip or two of water and a bite or two of food when my Widow wasn't looking. But by morning, I was back in the zone and dreaming of my fame as Amazing Cally, the cat who did the unthinkable.

Landing in Virginia

On Day Two, we crossed into Virginia and entered a world of split rail fences, rolling green pastures, and steaming temperatures. I was entering my new home state like an Olympic champion, ready to receive the Gold for my incredible two-day fast. As I emerged from my Cat Carrier, I looked around for the TV anchors who surely must have been following us. Finding none, I went for my food dish and chowed down. The press had missed their moment ... as they usually do. They may have been distracted by some other earth-shaking event.

When I looked about at my new home, once again it was boxes and chairs and chaos. But the bed was set up, so my Widow and I had a place to sleep in the midst of mayhem. I recognized some familiar smells so I settled right in and dreamed of new adventures in the land of Washington and Jefferson and Colonial Williamsburg.

Grits

My Northern friends had advised me the move South would introduce me to grits. They failed to mention what a grit looked like, so I began looking for one behind every door and in dark corners. I asked Precious, the Senior Cat Advisor to The World At Large, but she only replied ... Hmmmm ... which meant she didn't have a clue what a grit looked like or where to find one. So I continued my grit hunt on my own, hoping to bump into one and introduce myself in a casual way.

Flies, Spiders and Wasps

I was totally unprepared to be ambushed in my new living room by a squadron of houseflies. What to do? The lead fly looked menacing, somewhat like the Red Baron. I called for help, and my Widow came to the rescue with something she called a fly swatter. She whacked the daylights out of my tormentors, and we thought the worst was over.

Then a giant spider strolled into the kitchen, seeming to own the place. He had the body half the size of my paw and hairy black legs too numerous to count. My Widow spotted him almost as soon as I did and wound up her swatter. He dove for the underside of the refrigerator and waited her out. I sighted him next headed toward the bookcases, but he disappeared between the World Almanac and War and Peace.

We are now dropping cotton squares dowsed in peppermint oil behind the bookcases to drive him out. People who know spiders insist they will pull up stakes and go elsewhere to escape the smell of peppermint. I plan to patrol the area in case the peppermint theory doesn't work.

But life is never dull after the construction crew leaves and the windows are closed. That black spot on the ceiling that looks like dirt is now moving, up and down, over, and round and round. My attention is glued to the spot, and my Widow is watching me watching it. Neither of us know what we are watching...until the black spot moves down to her eye level.

Wasp, she murmurs, reaching for her swatter. I have no idea what a wasp is, but I'm ready for the challenge. Swat. Swat. I have done my part as the pointer, and she has done hers as the swatter.

I Must Admit...

Life in New Hampshire was a stroll in the park compared to life in Virginia. My Widow and I have separate quarters, with a door between us and the Main House. Yet she is quite out of breath trying to keep pace with life on the other side of the door. Busy adult grandchildren coming and going to summer jobs. Lively great-grands coming to visit, numerous friends and family who come and go, and constant cell phone activity.

Of course, being the only four-legged creature on the plantation, I am the main attraction. The great-grands love me because I'm soft, furry, and beautiful. They want to feed me whenever they see me. And they expect me to leap about at a moment's notice when they dangle red yarn and feather toys before me.

I am thinking of posting a "Cat is Napping" sign on the door when I am napping … along with a bucket of cold water above the door for those who can't read and walk right in. For cats in my age bracket, 15 hours out of every 24 is set aside for sleeping and the rest for eating and leaping about. I believe that's reasonable.

Living in Central AC

Summer is a sizzler in the South. Deena warned me. She also explained that most of the natives have central air conditioning and hop from one air conditioned spot to the next when temperatures soar. Those who don't have central AC go shopping in stores that do, she explained, seeming to know.

When I heard our new place had central AC, I was thrilled. When I get overheated, I think sinister thoughts. There is a flip side, however, to this central AC business. All doors and windows stay closed. Which means I lose my screened front door. Plead as I may, I can't persuade my Widow to open the door for my pleasure. And even if she did, there is no screen.

There is also no fresh air to sniff at open windows. I'm still adjusting to that. Sigh. I guess I'll have to text Deena. Maybe she knows a way to have the best of both worlds.

Hair Advice for My Widow

My Widow is not blessed with a head covering of fur, like me, but with hair that is naturally fine and limp and exceedingly ornery to manage. Humidity is not her friend. In fact, her hair is so droopy in high humidity, it falls over her eyes, making it seem as though she has none. I suggested she might wear a baseball cap until September ... or get a crew cut. She gave me "the look" and began looking for a miracle-working hairdresser who was also affordable.

Three phone calls later, she made an appointment on a friend-of-a-friend's recommendation, and roared off to a home salon, hoping for a humidity cure. The hairdresser lived in a rustic area, down a long lane, and greeted my Widow wrapped in a bath towel. She was just out of the shower, she explained, having been SO busy mowing her tall grass she had lost track of time. Just give her a minute, she said apologetically.

Meanwhile a gray parrot filled the silence with mystical remarks that sounded quite human, and a black cat grumped about having to give up the shampoo chair. Not being present, I can only theorize the place had no AC and the cat was a bit owlish because of the heat.

I heard the hairdresser knew her stuff, had lots of experience with limp hair, and told entertaining stories about her new wolf cub named "Bear." Meantime, my Widow's hair was teased and curled and backcombed to perfection while free range chickens ambled by the open front door en route to the vegetable garden. The whole process took about 45 minutes and every hair stayed in place for almost 24 hours. Then it drooped and flopped as before.

I tried cheering up my Widow With Drooping Hair by reminding her it was a fun time with a wonderful lady who described herself as pure "country," but I really think she should give serious consideration to wearing a baseball cap until September, or getting a crew cut.

The Other Side of the Door

The most amazing smells come from the other side of the door at our new house. I hate to brag, but being a cat gives me an awesome advantage over humans in detecting smells. There's a kitchen beyond the door, and my nose tells me there's a marvelous cook and a food paradise. I shiver with anticipation and park myself at the door's edge to get a better whiff when someone comes and goes. Sometimes I am invited in. But only on rare occasions.

The problem is my dander. There's a lovely teenager on the other side of the door who has breathing problems related to my dander. I can't imagine why. Dander is dander, and mine is quite ordinary, run-of-the-mill stuff.

I gave this some serious thought and finally decided to email Oliver and find out what he knows about dander transplants. I hear humans are always having things transplanted, so why not cats?

I am thinking of an organic dander transplant. One that is absolutely harmless to humans. If that doesn't do it, I could go for total dander removal. Humans get body parts removed all the time, so why not cats?

If I can solve the dander problem, then we might have an open door policy, and I would be free to prowl about in all the nooks and crannies of the Main House at my leisure. Including, of course, the kitchen of wonderful smells.

My Secret Place

In my house up North, there were endless possibilities for hiding out. Seven rooms with three beds to hide under, numerous chairs and then a basement and a garage. Now the field has narrowed. Two rooms and a large storage area (with double doors) that is only available when I sneak in. It's an easy maneuver because my Widow usually has her mind on settling in and not my whereabouts. If I keep a sharp lookout, I can duck in and disappear before she notices.

The other night, however, she didn't come back to storage when I planned, and I feared I would have to spend the night there all alone. Perhaps with spiders. So, being resourceful, I rattled the door. She mistook the noise for a home invasion and was about to call 911 when I spoke out in my larger-than-life voice and was released.

During the great-grands visits in the early weeks when I needed a secret place to hide, I went under the sofa. Quick and easy. Much too easy, it seems, as I was quickly discovered. No privacy. None whatsoever.

Come to think of it, even my litter box is public, not having a privacy door like humans have. The best I can do with such an embarrassment is sit facing the wall.

Mixed with the desire for privacy is the issue of self worth. I hate being taken for granted. I want to be missed, sought after, and worried about. I want to stroll casually into the room with wide-eyed innocence and say, "I had no idea you were looking for me. I have been right here all the time." Snicker. Snicker.

Actually, I now have found that perfect hiding place in my new house, and I only appear publicly when I feel like it. My Widow has spent hours on her hands and knees looking under things and behind things for me, and I shamelessly enjoy every minute of her frustration. After all, doesn't she disappear out the door for hours on end and never tell me where she is going or when she will return?

The Day My Widow Went To The DMV

A prime example of this disappearing act is the day my Widow went to the DMV. She had to get a Virginia driver's license. It's not easy to do. They want proof she was born, even though she stood before them in the flesh. A hospital birth certificate wasn't enough. They had to have official papers from the bureaucracy in the state of her birth.

I heard her say the process was long and complicated. There were security questions to be answered. Money had to be exchanged. Patience had to be exercised. I wouldn't be surprised if there are even secret handshakes. When I told Precious about this, she told me the DMV is misnamed. She thinks it should really be FADFS... Frustration and Delay For Sure.

Precious also pointed out that cats don't have to be licensed for anything. We roam free and go wherever we want without money being exchanged and security questions. No one owns us. We are free spirits. And there are no secret handshakes. I think cats have a superior life.

My New Name

My Widow now calls me the Four A.M. Cat. What she means is I meow her into consciousness nearly every morning at 4:00 and act starved. I really think I'm doing her a favor. She needs to stretch her muscles, move a bit. Cats KNOW it's not good to be motionless for long periods of time. Rule #2 in the Cat Manuel says we should stretch often, change positions often, arch our backs, and hence keep ourselves limber and youthful. It's our beauty secret.

So the 4:00 A.M. meow serves a dual purpose. My Widow gets up, she stretches, and she heads for her own private litter box. Being three-quarters awake after all that, she usually decides to feed me an early morning snack. Then she is even more awake, so she reads her morning devotions, checks her email and texts, and reads a bit more before dropping off to sleep again for another two hours or so. That's our morning routine. Works for me. I get a pre-breakfast breakfast, and being called the Four A.M. Cat is something I can live with.

Just for the record, I prefer to be called by my proper name ... Cally. Or maybe ... "Gorgeous," referring to my coloring. But I really don't want to hear anything like, "Hey You with the Whiskers!" That's totally uncivilized.

The Belly Display

"Gorgeous" is usually what I hear when I roll over on my back, stretch out my hind legs, draw up my front paws, and display my amazing multi-colored calico belly. My Widow oohs. She aahs.

Often she can't resist touching my magnificent underside. Sometimes I let her give it a pat. Sometimes I don't. It depends on my mood. After all, I am completely vulnerable in that full body stretch and sometimes I have second thoughts about being so defenseless. She is bigger than me and not totally trustworthy.

I am remembering the times she has stepped on me when we were waltzing around my food dish in the kitchen. She said I was under her feet and claimed to be sorry. I accepted her apology … somewhat.

However, she is the hand that feeds me and scoops my litter box, so I can afford to be reasonably tolerant.

One thing is sure. I wouldn't do the classic belly display for everyone. Certainly not for a stranger. It's reserved for a housemate or someone who has the "Trustworthy Seal of Approval."

Boo, Bones, and Deena Make a Move

I'm not the only one to make a move. Boo and her sisters also relocated, but only to a neighboring town, not across state lines like me. Boo tells me she was terrified. Deep voices, loud noises, strange vibrations. And then blankets covering everyone's carrier. What was happening? She was the youngest of the three, and like me, inexperienced in moves that sweep the room of furniture and everything else in sight.

Hours later, when her carrier finally popped open, things looked familiar. Somewhat. At least the bed she saw was the same old bed she and her sisters knew and loved. It smelled familiar. But the rest of the room was different. Not to worry, was Deena's advice. Things will "come right," she said, as if she knew.

Then the strange thing happened. Their Mama human completely disappeared. It wasn't like the condo when she closed the door and left them on their own for Empty House Time. There was no sound of a door closing. Just the sound of a can opener grinding away and faraway voices.

From the depths of "somewhere," their Mama's voice called them all to come "downstairs" for dinner. Downstairs? What could that mean? What was a "downstairs?" Nobody knew the answer. Not even Deena, the wise one. So with fear and trembling, they circled the bedroom and waited. Better to starve than to face the unknown.

A day passed ... without food. Finally hunger trumped fear for Boo, and she ventured into the unknown. She says she saw a strange tunnel-looking thing outside the bedroom, and screwing up her courage, slowly descended downward, one step at a time. At the bottom she found something familiar – a kitchen counter! Then food!

When Boo failed to return, Deena went sniffing for her and made the same descent and the same amazing discovery. Bones, however, stayed put under the bed. Boo suspects she got room service until her fear backed off.

It's hard to believe that in all Deena's vast experience she had never lived in a house with "stairs"… whereas my first house had two sets of them. In fact, I got my exercise trotting up and down both sets numerous times every day. If only they had asked me, I could have explained "stairs" and saved them from "fear of the unknown," not to mention near starvation.

I feel so smug. Of course, there's a flip side. Now they all find it wonderful to chase each other up and down the "stairs," while I have to invent my own exercise in my new one-story house.

Introducing Pippin, My Southern Friend

Pippin is a new friend who lives in North Carolina. One of his specialties is hunting. He travels to and fro thru a cat door, so he's not confined to indoor hunts like some of us. He displays his catches in a special place of an all-purpose room, called the "kill corner". He always waits nearby to bask in his family's applause and adoration.

Into this "kill corner" Pippin has dragged the usual assortment of mice and chipmunks. One day even a squirrel. He knew, however, he was meant for bigger things. Sure enough. He tracked down a rabbit, roughly his own size, and somehow "did it in". When his teenage human found the rabbit, stiff as a starched shirt in the kill corner, her scream of surprise was a show stopper.

But the mystery is this: How did Pippin get his rabbit thru the cat door? I haven't yet seen a cat door big enough for both a cat and a rabbit to go thru. Have you? Pippin only smiles the classic cat smile when asked how he did it … which means, he isn't telling … ever.

Scooter Also Isn't Telling...Ever

Just when I thought I had heard it all, along comes Scooter, a friend of a friend here in Virginia, who may be psychic. Scooter also has a reputation as a mighty hunter, an indoor and outdoor cat like Pippin. He could be counted on to tidy up the neighborhood of its overpopulation of mice, moles, and an occasional rabbit, but he was also a "cuddler" with great insight.

His Mistress will never forget his most amazing act of wrapping himself around her neck ... to announce her pregnancy, even before the doctor told her the news. Imagine that! Scooter took time out of his busy day to make this advance announcement and to assure her he would be there for her for the next nine months. All the way. No matter what.

She thoroughly enjoyed his companionship, even though she had no idea how he knew what he knew. When the baby was born and brought home for viewing, Scooter considered his job finished and went back to tidying up the neighborhood of mice and moles.

A year or so went by, then came another unexpected neck wrap with his Mistress. Sure enough. Scooter knew what he knew. Baby #2 was on the way.

When the same thing happened a third time, Scooter's Mistress didn't hesitate. She took the bassinet out of storage and called her doctor to tell him the news.

How did Scooter know these things? He only smiled the classic cat smile when asked how he knew what he knew ... which means, he isn't telling ... ever.

Pippin and Elsa

Pippin, the mighty hunter, is also known to be protective toward the females he lives among... like Elsa, the shy and sweet-tempered feline who occasionally uses the cat door to tour the yard and explore the nearby woods. Trouble is, Elsa has a poor sense of direction and needs help finding her way back. Pippin feels responsible for rounding her up and bringing her home.

As payment for his search and rescue service, he claims the privilege of plopping down on papers and books and jigsaw puzzles anywhere he finds them in the house ... especially when his humans are trying to work the puzzles or read the books.

In fact, he seems to wait until his ladies begin to read the book or work the puzzle before he decides to sit on it. It may be that he can't understand how anyone would find anything more entertaining than himself. Or it may be he discovered the warmth of paper at an early age and can't get enough of it.

The Cat Outside My Window

Hearing about Pippin's adventures, inside and out, is firing me up to get out the door of my new place and meet the fascinating cat that walks the neighborhood, seeming to know everything about everyone. The day my Widow and I moved in, this white cat with patches of black, came to call. Maybe a neighborly gesture to check me out. Maybe curiosity.

I'm curious, too. But, the best I can do with my "indoor" cat restrictions, is sit at my window and make eye contact. Certainly I would like to get better acquainted, as I miss Oliver and Max, my old neighborhood buddies up North. In my former home, there was a screen door, so conversation was possible, and Max was a great flirt, as well as a cat who gave good advice and brought news from far and wide. But with central air conditioning, there is no screen door and no open windows. All I can do is wiggle my ears, make non-threatening eye contact, or do slow blinks.

In case you're wondering, non-threatening eye contact is an on-again, off-again glance, not a confrontational stare. A slow blink is code for, "Let's be friends." Although sometimes it means, "I really like you." Yet "slow blinks" with a new acquaintance are more reserved, pending further developments.

Sneaking Out to Meet the Mystery Cat

I'm beyond thinking about sneaking out the door. I've already done it. It was a pre-planned move. I was waiting at the door and leaped with skill and grace over a basket my Widow was about to carry to the trash. This was followed by a quick dive under a car for cover. Alas, I was not quick enough. My tail betrayed me. I forgot to tuck it in, and as it was the only appendage available to her, she took hold of it and pulled me out from under.

She picked me up gingerly around my middle, avoiding my flaying claws, and put me back inside. I was deeply humiliated.

I have since recovered from my deep humiliation and am making future plans. Not a week goes by that I don't devise a new plot for sneaking out to meet the mystery cat. My Widow is no dummy. She reads me like a book. Now she waits until I am taking my afternoon nap to carry out the trash. And if an emergency arises, she exits the door with a shield of some sort protecting the opening.

We have had extended discussions about my obsession to bolt. I plead my case with every pathetic meow I can muster, as well as a mournful look. She bombards me with logic. "Cally," she says, "you have no idea what's out there. Do you think the security light goes on at night for no reason? No. It goes on because there is some animal prowling about. Probably hungry for cat thigh."

If I am not convinced, she looks me in the eye and asks, "What do you really know about your mystery cat? Not every cat is a protector, like Max, or Pippin, or Scooter."

Her most compelling argument is, "What would I do without you?" To tell the truth, I don't know what I would do without her either. We have become very congenial housemates. That is, she has grown used to my idiosyncrasies and I have grown used to hers. Besides I like snuggling on her covers on cold winter nights.

On the Other Hand ...

I have moments when all the logic in the world can't deter me from my instinct to BOLT and see WHAT'S OUT THERE IN THE BIG WORLD. I think I will contact Precious, Senior Advisor to The World At Large, to ask what she thinks. Maybe I will text Oliver to ask what he can find on the Internet. Maybe Deena has an opinion.

Or maybe I will go to my secret place where not even my Widow can find me and ponder on the wisdom of bolting.

I think I am having a midlife crisis.

CALLY'S WORD OF THANKS

I want to thank all my friends and their housemates for sharing their stories. I can assure you all the tales really happened. I may have added an editorial comment or two – but only when I couldn't help myself.

Special thanks to ...

Sally Humphries, the Widow who adopted me and wrote down everything I said and did. She lets me nap on her bed. She also feeds me and scoops me every day – for which I am eternally grateful.

Phyllis Brown and **Susie Baker**, who head my Fan Club and never seem to get enough of my stories. They both kept urging me to undertake this literary venture.

Hannah Knox, who did all the sketches in my book. After all, no one can capture everything in photos ... especially not Herbie's befuddled look after his time in the dryer.

Barbara Mouring and **Steve Mouring, Jr.** who seem to know all those computer things that totally befuddle me. They spent countless hours making me marketable.

Jane Lumsden, who gave so many hours of cell phone counsel. And would you believe, she is a dog lover, not a cat lover?

Lori Payne, who was my very creative graphic designer. She is also a dog lover, but didn't let my being a cat interfere with her work.

Kristie Morency, who is one of the dedicated Cat Rescuers of all time.

TRIBUTE TO CAT RESCUERS

Cally was only a one-pound ball of fur when she was dropped off on a rainy, slick road to fend for herself. She dodged cars in a frantic run for cover and crashed into a rickety fence where she cried her eyes out for her Mama ... who was permanently missing from action.

But a Cat Rescuer, one of those amazing people who would risk being rear-ended by a semi to rescue a cat in distress stopped to help. It's just that Cally wasn't buying. She was too scared to leave her rickety fence. The Cat Rescuer came back twice in the night to coax and sweet talk her. No sale. Finally in the morning the gentle Rescuer brought tuna, and Cally was seduced by the irresistible scent. Out she came and in she went – to a back pack. The rest is history.

Without Kristy Morency, the gentle and persistent Cat Rescuer – whose husband surely thought she was addled to go out not once, but twice in the night – this book would not have been possible.

THREE CHEERS FOR ALL THE CAT RESCUERS OF THE WORLD !

MAY THEIR NUMBER INCREASE!

Made in the USA
Middletown, DE
18 December 2019